PIANO • VOCAL • GUITAR

BROADWAY BALLADS

E 6 3

ISBN 0-7935-1446-0

HL®Hal Leonard Publishing Corporation

7777 West Bluemound Road P.O. Box 13819 Milwaukee, WI 53213

782.42/55
B

BROADWAY

BALLADS

AS LONG AS HE NEEDS ME

(From the Columbia Pictures - Romulus film "OLIVER!")

Words and Music by LIONEL BART

ALL I ASK OF YOU
(From "THE PHANTOM OF THE OPERA")

Music by ANDREW LLOYD WEBBER
Lyrics by CHARLES HART
Additional Lyrics by RICHARD STILGOE

BEWITCHED
(From "PAL JOEY")

Words by LORENZ HART
Music by RICHARD RODGERS

CAN'T HELP LOVIN' DAT MAN

(From "SHOW BOAT")

Words by OSCAR HAMMERSTEIN II
Music by JEROME KERN

COME RAIN OR COME SHINE
(From "ST. LOUIS WOMAN")

Words by JOHNNY MERCER
Music by HAROLD ARLEN

HOW ARE THINGS IN GLOCCA MORRA

(From "FINIAN'S RAINBOW")

Words by E.Y. HARBURG
Music by BURTON LANE

I CAN'T GET STARTED

(From "ZIEGFELD FOLLIES")

Words by IRA GERSHWIN
Music by VERNON DUKE

I DREAMED A DREAM

(From "LES MISERABLES")

Music by CLAUDE-MICHEL SCHÖNBERG
Lyrics by HERBERT KRETZMER
Original Text by ALAIN BOUBLIL AND JEAN-MARC NATEL

IF EVER I WOULD LEAVE YOU

(From "CAMELOT")

Words by ALAN JAY LERNER
Music by FREDERICK LOEWE

I HAVE DREAMED
(From "THE KING AND I")

Words by Oscar Hammerstein II
Music by Richard Rodgers

I'LL BE SEEING YOU
(From "RIGHT THIS WAY")

Words and Music by IRVING KAHAL
and SAMMY FAIN

I'VE GROWN ACCUSTOMED TO HER FACE
(From "MY FAIR LADY")

Words by ALAN JAY LERNER
Music by FREDERICK LOEWE

IF HE WALKED INTO MY LIFE
(From "MAME")

Music & Lyric by
JERRY HERMAN

IF I RULED THE WORLD
(From "PICKWICK")

Words by LESLIE BRICUSSE
Music by CYRIL ORNADEL

IF YOU REALLY KNEW ME

(From "THEY'RE PLAYING OUR SONG")

Words by CAROLE BAYER SAGER
Music by MARVIN HAMLISCH

* Female singers may substitute "he" wherever "you" appears.
Male singers may substitute "she" wherever "you" appears.

IT MIGHT AS WELL BE SPRING

(From "STATE FAIR")

Words by OSCAR HAMMERSTEIN II
Music by RICHARD RODGERS

LOST IN THE STARS
(From "LOST IN THE STARS")

Words by MAXWELL ANDERSON
Music by KURT WEILL

MAKE SOMEONE HAPPY

(From "DO RE MI")

Words by BETTY COMDEN and ADOLPH GREEN
Music by JULE STYNE

MR. WONDERFUL
(From the Musical "MR. WONDERFUL")

Words and Music by JERRY BOCK,
LARRY HOLOFCENER and GEORGE WEISS

MEMORY
(From "CATS")

Music by ANDREW LLOYD WEBBER
Text by TREVOR NUNN after T.S. ELIOT

THE MUSIC OF THE NIGHT

(From "THE PHANTOM OF THE OPERA")

Music by ANDREW LLOYD WEBBER
Lyrics by CHARLES HART
Additional Lyrics by RICHARD STILGOE

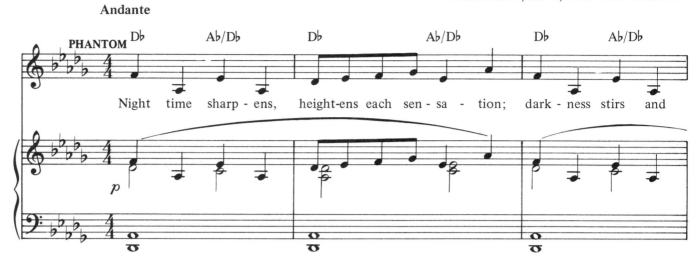

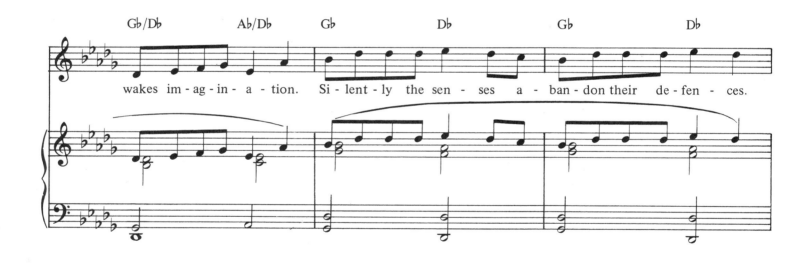

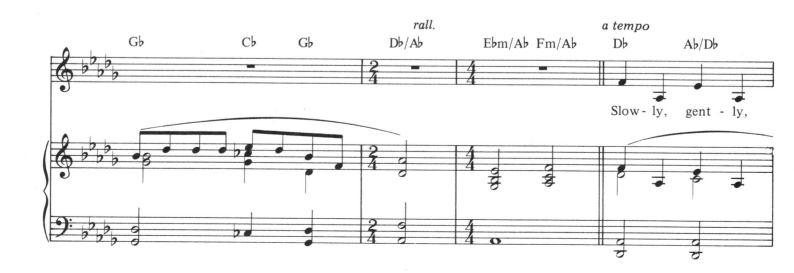

night un - furls its splen - dour; grasp it, sense it, trem - u - lous and ten - der.

Turn your face a - way from the gar - ish light of day, turn your thoughts a - way from cold, un - feel - ing

light and lis - ten to the mu - sic of the night. Close your eyes and sur - ren - der to your

dark - est dreams! Purge your thoughts of the life you knew be - fore! Close your

MY SHIP

(From the Musical Production "LADY IN THE DARK")

Words by IRA GERSHWIN
Music by KURT WEILL

MY FUNNY VALENTINE

(From "BABES IN ARMS")

Words by LORENZ HART
Music by RICHARD RODGERS

MY ROMANCE
(From "JUMBO")

Words by LORENZ HART
Music by RICHARD RODGERS

ON MY OWN
(From "LES MISERABLES")

Music by CLAUDE-MICHEL SCHÖNBERG
Lyrics by HERBERT KRETZMER, JOHN CAIRD and TREVOR NUNN
Original Text by ALAIN BOUBLIL and JEAN-MARC NATEL

94

Send In The Clowns
(From "A LITTLE NIGHT MUSIC")

Music and Lyrics by
STEPHEN SONDHEIM

THE PARTY'S OVER
(From "BELLS ARE RINGING")

Words by BETTY COMDEN & ADOLPH GREEN
Music by JULE STYNE

PEOPLE
(From "FUNNY GIRL")

Words by BOB MERRILL
Music by JULE STYNE

SEPTEMBER SONG
(From the Musical Play "KNICKERBOCKER HOLIDAY")

Words by MAXWELL ANDERSON
Music by KURT WEILL

SMOKE GETS IN YOUR EYES
(From "ROBERTA")

Words by OTTO HARBACH
Music by JEROME KERN

SUN AND MOON
(From "MISS SAIGON")

Music by CLAUDE-MICHEL SCHÖNBERG
Lyrics by RICHARD MALTBY JR. & ALAIN BOUBLIL
Adapted from original French Lyrics by ALAIN BOUBLIL

UNEXPECTED SONG
(From "SONG & DANCE")

Music by Andrew Lloyd Webber
Lyrics by Don Black

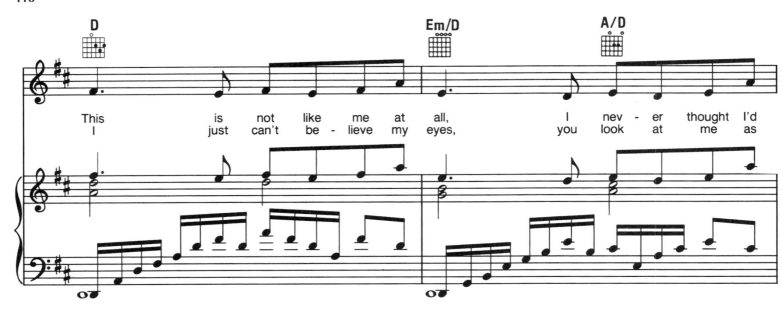

This is not like me at all, I nev-er thought I'd
I just can't be-lieve my eyes, you look at me as

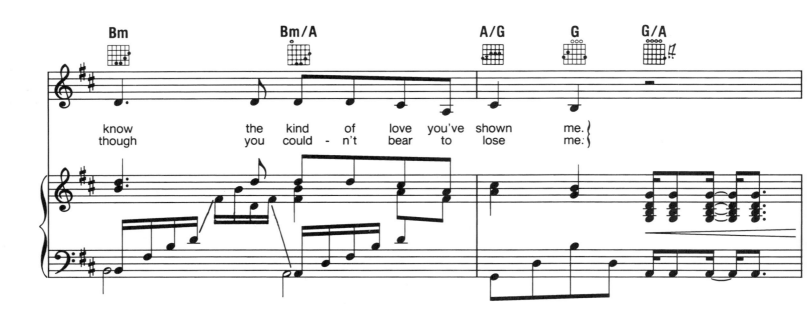

know the kind of love you've shown me.
though you kind could-n't bear to lose me.

Now no mat-ter where I am, no mat-ter what I do, I see your face ap-

thrown me. This is not like me at all, I nev-er thought I'd

know the kind of love you've shown me. Now no mat-ter where I

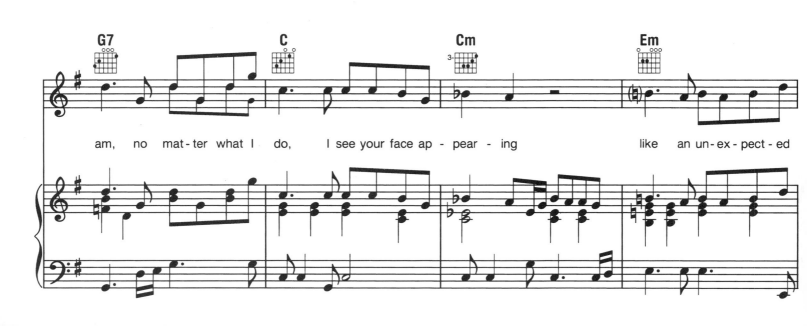

am, no mat-ter what I do, I see your face ap-pear-ing like an un-ex-pect-ed

TILL THERE WAS YOU

(From "THE MUSIC MAN")

Words and Music by
MEREDITH WILLSON

Lyrics:

There were bells ___ on a hill, ___ but I
birds ___ in the sky, ___ but I

nev-er ___ heard them ring-ing, ___ No, I nev-er heard them at
nev-er ___ saw them wing-ing, ___ No, I nev-er saw them at

WE KISS IN A SHADOW

(From "THE KING AND I")

Words by OSCAR HAMMERSTEIN II
Music by RICHARD RODGERS

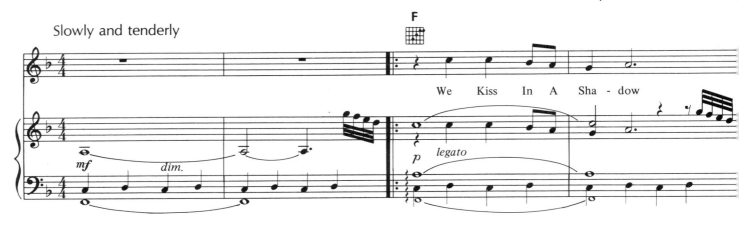

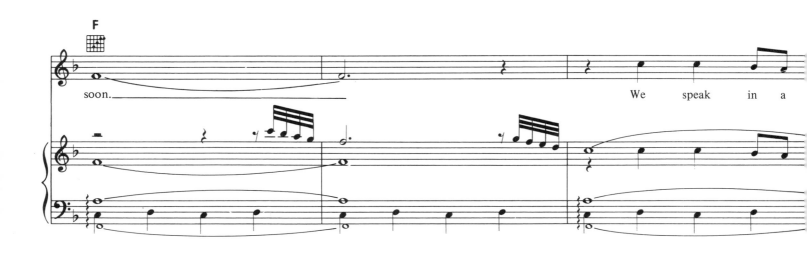

WHAT I DID FOR LOVE
(From "A CHORUS LINE")

Music by MARVIN HAMLISCH
Lyric by EDWARD KLEBAN

Slowly

Kiss to-day___ good-bye,___

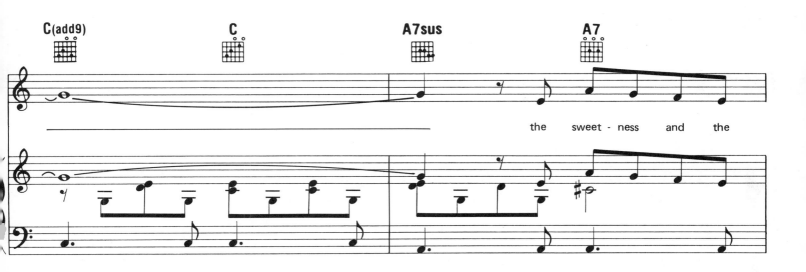

C(add9) C A7sus A7

the sweet-ness and the

Dm7 Fm

sor - row.___ Wish me luck,___ the

YOUNG AND FOOLISH
(From "PLAIN AND FANCY")

Words by ARNOLD B. HORWITT
Music by ALBERT HAGUE

MORE SONGS, MORE SHOWS...
MORE BROADWAY!

50 Broadway Shows/50 Broadway Songs
A beautiful collection that features the "highlight" song from 50 of the greatest Broadway shows ever! Includes: You'll Never Walk Alone • Memory • What I Did For Love • Sunrise, Sunset • People • Day By Day • Ol' Man River • and many more. Also includes an "About The Shows" section that gives fascinating trivia and facts about each show.
00359867 ....$14.95

The Best Broadway Songs Ever – Newly Revised
A truly golden collection of over 70 of Broadway's best, featuring: All I Ask Of You • Bewitched • Don't Cry For Me Argentina • I Dreamed A Dream • Love Changes Everything • Memory • Send In The Clowns • You'll Never Walk Alone • and more.
00309155 ....$15.95

Broadway! Volume One
Over 60 immortal show tunes, including: As Long As He Needs Me • Bali Ha'i • Camelot • Do-Re-Mi • Fanny • Get Me To The Church On Time • I Could Have Danced All Night.
00309240 ....$12.95

Broadway! Volume Two
72 more of Broadway's best, featuring: Let Me Entertain You • My Favorite Things • Oklahoma • Ol' Man River • On A Clear Day • Put On A Happy Face • The Sound Of Music • They Call The Wind Maria.
00309241 ....$12.95

Broadway Gold
100 show tunes from a wide variety of Broadway's biggest hits: Bess, You Is My Woman • C'est Magnifique • Do-Re-Mi • Happy Talk • I Love Paris • I Whistle A Happy Tune • The Lady Is A Tramp • Let Me Entertain You • Memory • My Funny Valentine • Oklahoma • Old Devil Moon • The Rain In Spain • Soon It's Gonna Rain • Some Enchanted Evening • When I Fall In Love • Young And Foolish • Give A Little Whistle • I Ain't Down Yet • I've Got Your Number • It Only Takes A Moment • Mame • Seventy-Six Trombones • Standing On The Corner • Summer Nights • Till There Was You • Tomorrow • What I Did For Love • Put On A Happy Face • The Night They Invented Champagne • Silk Stockings • There Is Nothin' Like A Dame • many more.
00361396 ....$16.95

Broadway Overtures For Piano
The first major collection of Broadway overtures ever offered. Each selection is a piano reduction of the authentic material.

Volume 1 – Shows include: Camelot • Carousel • The Fantasticks • Oklahoma! • South Pacific • and six more.
00359441 ....$9.95

Volume 2 – Shows include: Funny Girl • The King And I • On A Clear Day You Can See Forever • Showboat • and 10 more.
00359442 ....$9.95

Broadway Platinum – Ultimate Series
100 more popular Broadway songs, featuring hits like: A Fellow Needs A Girl • As Long As He Needs Me • Button Up Your Overcoat • Everything's Coming Up Roses • Funny Girl • Gigi • Hello, Young Lovers • My Favorite Things • People • Try To Remember • A Wonderful Guy • many more.
00311495 Comb-bound $19.95
00311496 Stay-Open Binding $16.95

Comedy Songs From Broadway Musicals
17 humorous songs made famous in such fantastic Broadway shows as: Guys and Dolls • Kiss Me Kate • South Pacific • A Funny Thing Happened On The Way To The Forum • Bye Bye Birdie • Showboat • and more. Also includes an introduction by noted historian Stanley Green, as well as a brief narrative on each song.
00359489 ....$9.95

The Definitive Broadway Collection
This is simply the best and most comprehensive collection of Broadway music ever arranged in a piano/vocal format! 142 of the greatest show tunes compiled into one volume. Comb-bound for easy use – this is one book that every Broadway lover must have! Songs include: Don't Cry For Me Argentina • Edelweiss • Hello Dolly! • I Could Have Danced All Night • I Dreamed A Dream • I Know Him So Well • Lullabye Of Broadway • Mack The Knife • Somewhere • Summertime • Sunrise, Sunset • Tomorrow • more.
00359570 ....$27.95

The Ultimate Broadway Fake Book – revised
More than 650 songs from fabulous Broadway shows. Melodies, lyrics, chords. For piano, organ, guitar and all "C" instruments. Sturdy plastic comb binding. Shows include: Annie • Cabaret • Fiddler On The Roof • The King And I • La Cage Aux Folles • Starlight Express • and more.
00240046 ....$29.95

For more information, see your local music dealer, or write to:
Hal Leonard Publishing Corporation
P.O. Box 13819 Milwaukee, Wisconsin 53213